CHURCH NOTES JOURNAL

a weekly sermon & bible class notebook for kids

written & designed by Shalana Frisby

123JOURNALIT.COM

Get organized for success in your Bible study!
Download your bonus free printables now:

WWW.123JOURNALIT.COM / FREEBIES
SCRIPTURE FLASHCARDS - BIBLE READING PROMPTS - JOURNALING PAGES

More information at: www.123journalit.com

First Printing: February 2018
1 2 3 Journal It Publishing

ISBN-13: 978-1-947209-22-0
Bright Stars Cover Edition

Weekly Bible Reading Record

DATES	BOOKS, CHAPTERS, and VERSES

Monthly Church Attendance and Goals

MONTH: _____

attendance dates:
- ☐ _____
- ☐ _____
- ☐ _____
- ☐ _____
- ☐ _____

monthly goals:
_____
_____
_____
_____
_____
_____

MONTH: _____

attendance dates:
- ☐ _____
- ☐ _____
- ☐ _____
- ☐ _____
- ☐ _____

monthly goals:
_____
_____
_____
_____
_____
_____

MONTH: _____

attendance dates:
- ☐ _____
- ☐ _____
- ☐ _____
- ☐ _____
- ☐ _____

monthly goals:
_____
_____
_____
_____
_____
_____

MONTH: _____

attendance dates:
- ☐ _____
- ☐ _____
- ☐ _____
- ☐ _____
- ☐ _____

monthly goals:
_____
_____
_____
_____
_____
_____

MONTH: _____

attendance dates:
- ☐ _____
- ☐ _____
- ☐ _____
- ☐ _____
- ☐ _____

monthly goals:
_____
_____
_____
_____
_____
_____

MONTH: _____

attendance dates:
- ☐ _____
- ☐ _____
- ☐ _____
- ☐ _____
- ☐ _____

monthly goals:
_____
_____
_____
_____
_____
_____

WORSHIP SERVICE HAPPENINGS

List some songs from today:

_____

_____

_____

Write a scripture you heard:

_____

_____

_____

Who needs prayer this week?

_____

_____

_____

What are some upcoming events?

_____

_____

PLACE:

_____

_____

date

SERMON NOTES

SPEAKER:

What is today's sermon about?

_____

_____

_____

_____

_____

Where is it in the Bible?

_____

_____

_____

_____

BIBLE CLASS LESSON

TEACHER:

Write about what you learned:

_____

_____

_____

_____

_____

How can what you learned help you?

_____

_____

_____

_____

Name a person who helped you today:

What did they do?

Write something funny or interesting you heard today.

Draw something you learned about today:

8

WEEKLY STUDY NOTES

_____

_____

_____

_____

_____

_____

_____

_____

_____

_____

_____

_____

_____

_____

_____

PONDER . . . DOODLE . . . DRAW

WORSHIP SERVICE HAPPENINGS

List some songs from today:

_____

_____

_____

Write a scripture you heard:

_____

_____

_____

Who needs prayer this week?

_____

_____

_____

What are some upcoming events?

_____

_____

_____

PLACE:

_____

_____

date

SERMON NOTES

SPEAKER:

What is today's sermon about?

_____

_____

_____

_____

_____

Where is it in the Bible?

_____

_____

_____

_____

BIBLE CLASS LESSON

TEACHER:

Write about what you learned:

_____

_____

_____

_____

_____

How can what you learned help you?

_____

_____

_____

_____

Write something funny or interesting you heard today.

Name a person who helped you today:

What did they do?

Draw something you learned about today:

WEEKLY STUDY NOTES

PONDER . . . DOODLE . . . DRAW

WORSHIP SERVICE HAPPENINGS

List some songs from today:

_____
_____
_____

Write a scripture you heard:

_____
_____
_____

Who needs prayer this week?

_____
_____
_____

What are some upcoming events?

_____
_____
_____

PLACE:

_____
_____

date

SERMON NOTES

SPEAKER:

What is today's sermon about?

_____
_____
_____
_____
_____

Where is it in the Bible?

_____
_____
_____
_____

BIBLE CLASS LESSON

TEACHER:

Write about what you learned:

_____

_____

_____

_____

_____

How can what you learned help you?

_____

_____

_____

_____

Name a person who helped you today:

What did they do?

Write something funny or interesting you heard today.

Draw something you learned about today:

WEEKLY STUDY NOTES

PONDER ... DOODLE ... DRAW

WORSHIP SERVICE HAPPENINGS

List some songs from today:

_____

_____

_____

Write a scripture you heard:

_____

_____

_____

Who needs prayer this week?

_____

_____

_____

What are some upcoming events?

_____

_____

_____

PLACE:

_____

_____

date

SERMON NOTES

SPEAKER:

What is today's sermon about?

_____

_____

_____

_____

_____

Where is it in the Bible?

_____

_____

_____

BIBLE CLASS LESSON

TEACHER:

Write about what you learned:

_____

_____

_____

_____

_____

How can what you learned help you?

_____

_____

_____

_____

Write something funny or interesting you heard today.

Name a person who helped you today:

What did they do?

Draw something you learned about today:

WEEKLY STUDY NOTES

PONDER . . . DOODLE . . . DRAW

WORSHIP SERVICE HAPPENINGS

List some songs from today:

_____

_____

_____

Write a scripture you heard:

_____

_____

_____

Who needs prayer this week?

_____

_____

_____

What are some upcoming events?

_____

_____

PLACE:

_____

_____

date

SERMON NOTES

SPEAKER:

What is today's sermon about?

_____

_____

_____

_____

_____

Where is it in the Bible?

_____

_____

_____

BIBLE CLASS LESSON

TEACHER:

Write about what you learned:

_____

_____

_____

_____

_____

How can what you learned help you?

_____

_____

_____

_____

Write something funny or interesting you heard today.

Name a person who helped you today:

What did they do?

Draw something you learned about today:

WEEKLY STUDY NOTES

PONDER ... DOODLE ... DRAW

WORSHIP SERVICE HAPPENINGS

List some songs from today:

_____

_____

_____

Write a scripture you heard:

_____

_____

_____

Who needs prayer this week?

_____

_____

_____

What are some upcoming events?

_____

_____

PLACE:

_____

_____

date

SERMON NOTES

SPEAKER:

What is today's sermon about?

_____

_____

_____

_____

_____

Where is it in the Bible?

_____

_____

_____

BIBLE CLASS LESSON

TEACHER:

Write about what you learned:

_____

_____

_____

_____

_____

How can what you learned help you?

_____

_____

_____

_____

Name a person who helped you today:

What did they do?

Write something funny or interesting you heard today.

Draw something you learned about today:

WEEKLY STUDY NOTES

PONDER . . . DOODLE . . . DRAW

WORSHIP SERVICE HAPPENINGS

List some songs from today:

_____

_____

_____

Write a scripture you heard:

_____

_____

_____

Who needs prayer this week?

_____

_____

_____

What are some upcoming events?

_____

_____

_____

PLACE:

_____

_____

date

SERMON NOTES

SPEAKER:

What is today's sermon about?

_____

_____

_____

_____

_____

_____

Where is it in the Bible?

_____

_____

_____

BIBLE CLASS LESSON

TEACHER:

Write about what you learned:

_____

_____

_____

_____

_____

How can what you learned help you?

_____

_____

_____

_____

Write something funny or interesting you heard today.

Name a person who helped you today:

What did they do?

Draw something you learned about today:

32

WEEKLY STUDY NOTES

PONDER . . . DOODLE . . . DRAW

WORSHIP SERVICE HAPPENINGS

List some songs from today:

_____

_____

_____

Write a scripture you heard:

_____

_____

_____

Who needs prayer this week?

_____

_____

_____

What are some upcoming events?

_____

_____

_____

PLACE:

_____

_____

date

SERMON NOTES

SPEAKER:

What is today's sermon about?

_____

_____

_____

_____

_____

Where is it in the Bible?

_____

_____

_____

_____

BIBLE CLASS LESSON

TEACHER:

Write about what you learned:

_____

_____

_____

_____

_____

How can what you learned help you?

_____

_____

_____

_____

Write something funny or interesting you heard today.

Name a person who helped you today:

What did they do?

Draw something you learned about today:

36

WEEKLY STUDY NOTES

_____

_____

_____

_____

_____

_____

_____

_____

_____

_____

_____

_____

_____

_____

_____

PONDER . . . DOODLE . . . DRAW

WORSHIP SERVICE HAPPENINGS

List some songs from today:

_____

_____

_____

Write a scripture you heard:

_____

_____

_____

Who needs prayer this week?

_____

_____

_____

What are some upcoming events?

_____

_____

_____

PLACE:

_____

_____

date

SERMON NOTES

SPEAKER:

What is today's sermon about?

_____

_____

_____

_____

_____

Where is it in the Bible?

_____

_____

_____

_____

BIBLE CLASS LESSON

TEACHER:

Write about what you learned:

_____

_____

_____

_____

_____

How can what you learned help you?

_____

_____

_____

_____

Write something funny or interesting you heard today.

Name a person who helped you today:

What did they do?

Draw something you learned about today:

WORSHIP SERVICE HAPPENINGS

List some songs from today:

_____

_____

_____

Write a scripture you heard:

_____

_____

_____

Who needs prayer this week?

_____

_____

_____

What are some upcoming events?

_____

_____

_____

PLACE:

_____

_____

date

SERMON NOTES

SPEAKER:

What is today's sermon about?

_____

_____

_____

_____

_____

_____

Where is it in the Bible?

_____

_____

_____

_____

BIBLE CLASS LESSON

TEACHER:

Write about what you learned:

_____

_____

_____

_____

_____

How can what you learned help you?

_____

_____

_____

_____

Write something funny or interesting you heard today.

Name a person who helped you today:

What did they do?

Draw something you learned about today:

44

WEEKLY STUDY NOTES

_____

_____

_____

_____

_____

_____

_____

_____

_____

_____

_____

_____

_____

_____

PONDER . . . DOODLE . . . DRAW

WORSHIP SERVICE HAPPENINGS

List some songs from today:

_____

_____

_____

Write a scripture you heard:

_____

_____

_____

Who needs prayer this week?

_____

_____

_____

What are some upcoming events?

_____

_____

PLACE:

_____

_____

date

SERMON NOTES

SPEAKER:

What is today's sermon about?

_____

_____

_____

_____

_____

Where is it in the Bible?

_____

_____

_____

BIBLE CLASS LESSON

TEACHER:

Write about what you learned:

_____

_____

_____

_____

_____

How can what you learned help you?

_____

_____

_____

_____

Name a person who helped you today:

What did they do?

Write something funny or interesting you heard today.

Draw something you learned about today:

_____

_____

_____

_____

_____

_____

_____

_____

_____

_____

_____

_____

_____

_____

_____

_____

WORSHIP SERVICE HAPPENINGS

List some songs from today:

_____

_____

_____

Write a scripture you heard:

_____

_____

_____

Who needs prayer this week?

_____

_____

_____

What are some upcoming events?

_____

_____

_____

PLACE:

_____

_____

date

SERMON NOTES

SPEAKER:

What is today's sermon about?

_____

_____

_____

_____

_____

Where is it in the Bible?

_____

_____

_____

BIBLE CLASS LESSON

TEACHER:

Write about what you learned:

_____

_____

_____

_____

_____

How can what you learned help you?

_____

_____

_____

_____

Write something funny or interesting you heard today.

Name a person who helped you today:

What did they do?

Draw something you learned about today:

52

WEEKLY STUDY NOTES

_____

_____

_____

_____

_____

_____

_____

_____

_____

_____

_____

_____

_____

_____

PONDER ... DOODLE ... DRAW

WORSHIP SERVICE HAPPENINGS

List some songs from today:

_____

_____

_____

Write a scripture you heard:

_____

_____

_____

Who needs prayer this week?

_____

_____

_____

What are some upcoming events?

_____

_____

_____

PLACE:

_____

_____

date

SERMON NOTES

SPEAKER:

What is today's sermon about?

_____

_____

_____

_____

_____

_____

Where is it in the Bible?

_____

_____

_____

_____

BIBLE CLASS LESSON

TEACHER:

Write about what you learned:

_____

_____

_____

_____

_____

How can what you learned help you?

_____

_____

_____

_____

Write something funny or interesting you heard today.

Name a person who helped you today:

What did they do?

Draw something you learned about today:

WEEKLY STUDY NOTES

_____

_____

_____

_____

_____

_____

_____

_____

_____

_____

_____

_____

_____

_____

PONDER . . . DOODLE . . . DRAW

WORSHIP SERVICE HAPPENINGS

List some songs from today:

_____

_____

_____

Write a scripture you heard:

_____

_____

_____

Who needs prayer this week?

_____

_____

_____

What are some upcoming events?

_____

_____

_____

PLACE:

_____

_____

date

SERMON NOTES

SPEAKER:

What is today's sermon about?

_____

_____

_____

_____

_____

Where is it in the Bible?

_____

_____

_____

_____

BIBLE CLASS LESSON

TEACHER:

Write about what you learned:

_____
_____
_____
_____
_____

How can what you learned help you?

_____
_____
_____
_____

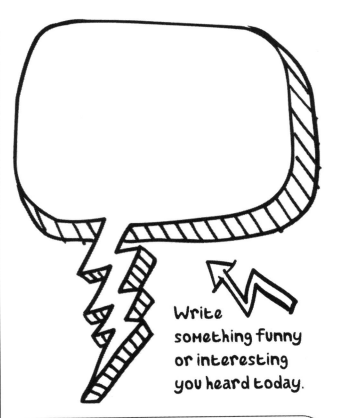

Write something funny or interesting you heard today.

Draw something you learned about today:

Name a person who helped you today:

What did they do?

WORSHIP SERVICE HAPPENINGS

List some songs from today:

_____

_____

_____

Write a scripture you heard:

_____

_____

_____

Who needs prayer this week?

_____

_____

_____

What are some upcoming events?

_____

_____

_____

PLACE:

_____

_____

date

SERMON NOTES

SPEAKER:

What is today's sermon about?

_____

_____

_____

_____

_____

Where is it in the Bible?

_____

_____

_____

BIBLE CLASS LESSON

TEACHER:

Write about what you learned:

_____

_____

_____

_____

_____

How can what you learned help you?

_____

_____

_____

_____

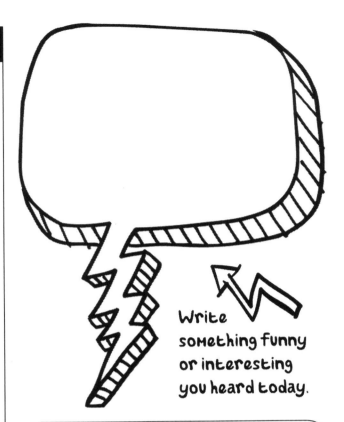

Write something funny or interesting you heard today.

Name a person who helped you today:

What did they do?

Draw something you learned about today:

WORSHIP SERVICE HAPPENINGS

List some songs from today:

_____

_____

_____

Write a scripture you heard:

_____

_____

_____

Who needs prayer this week?

_____

_____

_____

What are some upcoming events?

_____

_____

PLACE:

_____

_____

date

SERMON NOTES

SPEAKER:

What is today's sermon about?

_____

_____

_____

_____

_____

Where is it in the Bible?

_____

_____

_____

_____

_____

BIBLE CLASS LESSON

TEACHER:

Write about what you learned:

_____

_____

_____

_____

_____

How can what you learned help you?

_____

_____

_____

_____

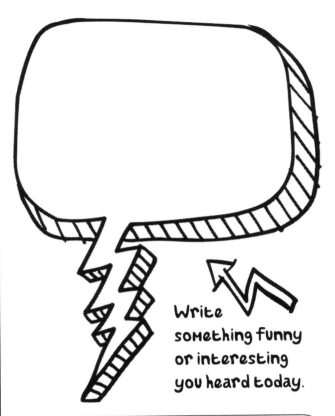

Write something funny or interesting you heard today.

Name a person who helped you today:

What did they do?

Draw something you learned about today:

WORSHIP SERVICE HAPPENINGS

List some songs from today:

_____
_____
_____

Write a scripture you heard:

_____
_____
_____

Who needs prayer this week?

_____
_____
_____

What are some upcoming events?

_____
_____

PLACE:

_____
_____

date

SERMON NOTES

SPEAKER:

What is today's sermon about?

_____
_____
_____
_____
_____

Where is it in the Bible?

_____
_____
_____
_____

BIBLE CLASS LESSON

TEACHER:

Write about what you learned:

_____

_____

_____

_____

_____

How can what you learned help you?

_____

_____

_____

_____

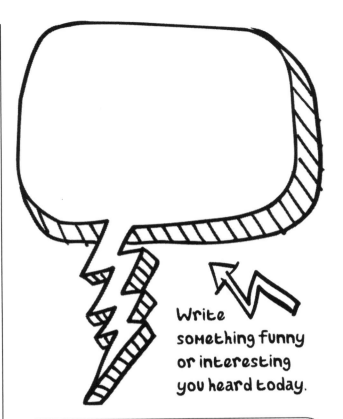

Write something funny or interesting you heard today.

Name a person who helped you today:

What did they do?

Draw something you learned about today:

WORSHIP SERVICE HAPPENINGS

List some songs from today:

_____

_____

_____

Write a scripture you heard:

_____

_____

_____

Who needs prayer this week?

_____

_____

_____

What are some upcoming events?

_____

_____

PLACE:

_____

_____

date

SERMON NOTES

SPEAKER:

What is today's sermon about?

_____

_____

_____

_____

_____

Where is it in the Bible?

_____

_____

_____

_____

BIBLE CLASS LESSON

TEACHER:

Write about what you learned:

_____

_____

_____

_____

_____

How can what you learned help you?

_____

_____

_____

_____

Name a person who helped you today:

What did they do?

Write something funny or interesting you heard today.

Draw something you learned about today:

WEEKLY STUDY NOTES

PONDER . . . DOODLE . . . DRAW

WORSHIP SERVICE HAPPENINGS

List some songs from today:

_____

_____

_____

Write a scripture you heard:

_____

_____

_____

Who needs prayer this week?

_____

_____

_____

What are some upcoming events?

_____

_____

_____

PLACE:

_____

_____

date

SERMON NOTES

SPEAKER:

What is today's sermon about?

_____

_____

_____

_____

_____

Where is it in the Bible?

_____

_____

_____

_____

BIBLE CLASS LESSON

TEACHER:

Write about what you learned:

_____

_____

_____

_____

_____

How can what you learned help you?

_____

_____

_____

_____

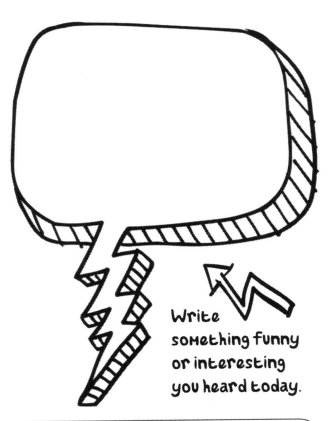

Write something funny or interesting you heard today.

Draw something you learned about today:

Name a person who helped you today:

What did they do?

WEEKLY STUDY NOTES

PONDER . . . DOODLE . . . DRAW

WORSHIP SERVICE HAPPENINGS

List some songs from today:

_____

_____

_____

Write a scripture you heard:

_____

_____

_____

Who needs prayer this week?

_____

_____

_____

What are some upcoming events?

_____

_____

_____

PLACE:

_____

_____

date

SERMON NOTES

SPEAKER:

What is today's sermon about?

_____

_____

_____

_____

_____

_____

Where is it in the Bible?

_____

_____

_____

_____

BIBLE CLASS LESSON

TEACHER:

Write about what you learned:

_____

_____

_____

_____

_____

How can what you learned help you?

_____

_____

_____

_____

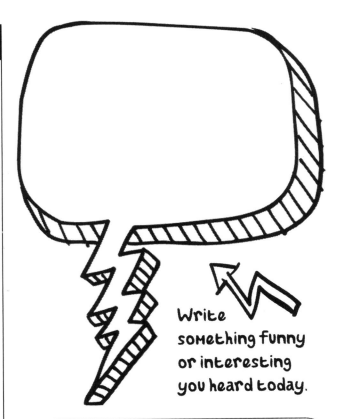

Write something funny or interesting you heard today.

Name a person who helped you today:

What did they do?

Draw something you learned about today:

WEEKLY STUDY NOTES

PONDER . . . DOODLE . . . DRAW

WORSHIP SERVICE HAPPENINGS

List some songs from today:

_____

_____

_____

Write a scripture you heard:

_____

_____

_____

Who needs prayer this week?

_____

_____

_____

What are some upcoming events?

_____

_____

PLACE:

_____

_____

date

SERMON NOTES

SPEAKER:

What is today's sermon about?

_____

_____

_____

_____

_____

_____

Where is it in the Bible?

_____

_____

_____

_____

BIBLE CLASS LESSON

TEACHER:

Write about what you learned:

_____

_____

_____

_____

_____

How can what you learned help you?

_____

_____

_____

_____

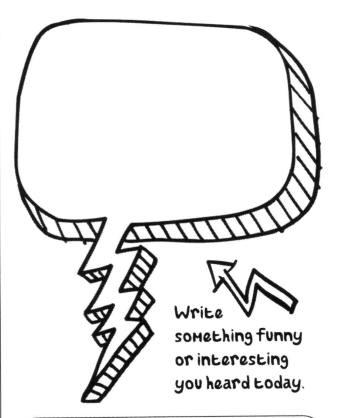

Write something funny or interesting you heard today.

Draw something you learned about today:

Name a person who helped you today:

What did they do?

WEEKLY STUDY NOTES

_____

_____

_____

_____

_____

_____

_____

_____

_____

_____

_____

_____

_____

PONDER ... DOODLE ... DRAW

WORSHIP SERVICE HAPPENINGS

List some songs from today:

_____

_____

_____

Write a scripture you heard:

_____

_____

_____

Who needs prayer this week?

_____

_____

_____

What are some upcoming events?

_____

_____

PLACE:

_____

_____

date

SERMON NOTES

SPEAKER:

What is today's sermon about?

_____

_____

_____

_____

_____

Where is it in the Bible?

_____

_____

_____

_____

BIBLE CLASS LESSON

TEACHER:

Write about what you learned:

_____

_____

_____

_____

_____

How can what you learned help you?

_____

_____

_____

_____

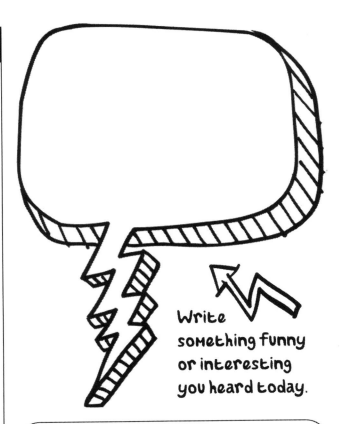

Write something funny or interesting you heard today.

Name a person who helped you today:

What did they do?

Draw something you learned about today:

WEEKLY STUDY NOTES

PONDER . . . DOODLE . . . DRAW

WORSHIP SERVICE HAPPENINGS

List some songs from today:

_____

_____

_____

Write a scripture you heard:

_____

_____

_____

Who needs prayer this week?

_____

_____

_____

What are some upcoming events?

_____

_____

PLACE:

_____

_____

date

SERMON NOTES

SPEAKER:

What is today's sermon about?

_____

_____

_____

_____

_____

Where is it in the Bible?

_____

_____

_____

_____

BIBLE CLASS LESSON

TEACHER:

Write about what you learned:

_____

_____

_____

_____

_____

How can what you learned help you?

_____

_____

_____

_____

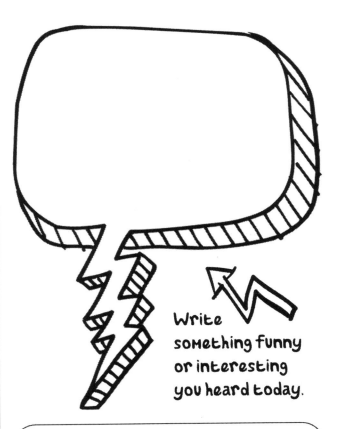

Write something funny or interesting you heard today.

Draw something you learned about today:

Name a person who helped you today:

What did they do?

WORSHIP SERVICE HAPPENINGS

List some songs from today:

_____

_____

_____

Write a scripture you heard:

_____

_____

_____

Who needs prayer this week?

_____

_____

_____

What are some upcoming events?

_____

_____

_____

PLACE:

_____

_____

date

SERMON NOTES

SPEAKER:

What is today's sermon about?

_____

_____

_____

_____

Where is it in the Bible?

_____

_____

_____

BIBLE CLASS LESSON

TEACHER:

Write about what you learned:

_____

_____

_____

_____

_____

How can what you learned help you?

_____

_____

_____

_____

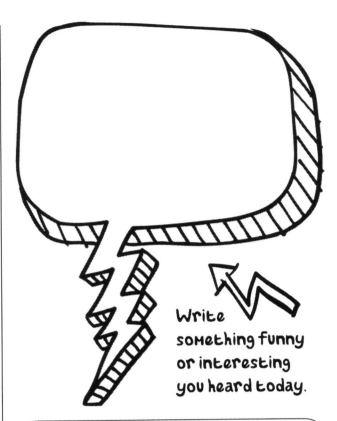

Write something funny or interesting you heard today.

Draw something you learned about today:

Name a person who helped you today:

What did they do?

WORSHIP SERVICE HAPPENINGS

List some songs from today:

_____

_____

_____

Write a scripture you heard:

_____

_____

_____

Who needs prayer this week?

_____

_____

_____

What are some upcoming events?

_____

_____

_____

PLACE:

_____

_____

date

SERMON NOTES

SPEAKER:

What is today's sermon about?

_____

_____

_____

_____

_____

_____

Where is it in the Bible?

_____

_____

_____

_____

BIBLE CLASS LESSON

TEACHER:

Write about what you learned:

_____

_____

_____

_____

_____

How can what you learned help you?

_____

_____

_____

_____

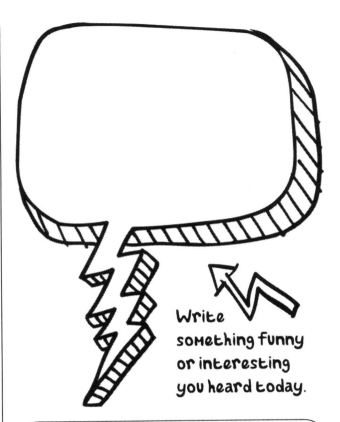

Write something funny or interesting you heard today.

Draw something you learned about today:

Name a person who helped you today:

What did they do?

WORSHIP SERVICE HAPPENINGS

List some songs from today:

_____

_____

_____

Write a scripture you heard:

_____

_____

_____

Who needs prayer this week?

_____

_____

_____

What are some upcoming events?

_____

_____

_____

PLACE:

_____

_____

date

SERMON NOTES

SPEAKER:

What is today's sermon about?

_____

_____

_____

_____

_____

Where is it in the Bible?

_____

_____

_____

_____

BIBLE CLASS LESSON

TEACHER:

Write about what you learned:

_____

_____

_____

_____

_____

How can what you learned help you?

_____

_____

_____

_____

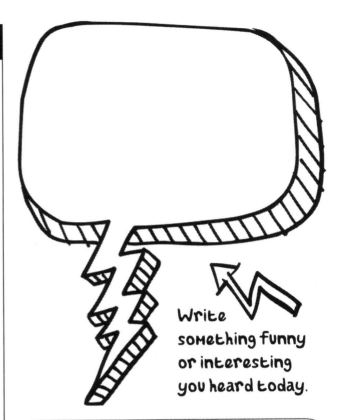

Write something funny or interesting you heard today.

Draw something you learned about today:

Name a person who helped you today:

What did they do?

Over 30 titles to choose from for all your Bible study & prayer journaling:

INDIVIDUALS - CHURCHES - PRIVATE SCHOOLS - HOMESCHOOLING

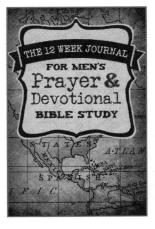

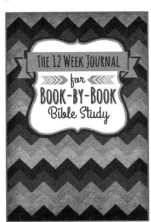

Made in the USA
Lexington, KY
12 December 2018